EDWIN MORGAN TWENTIES

LOVE

CELEBRATING EDWIN MORGAN'S CENTENARY

Love
Scotland
Menagerie
Take Heart
Space and Spaces

EDWIN MORGAN TWENTIES

LOVE

SELECTED POEMS

Introduced by
Jackie Kay

Polygon

in association with
Carcanet

First published in Great Britain in 2020 by
Polygon, an imprint of Birlinn Ltd, in association with
Carcanet Press Ltd

Birlinn Ltd
West Newington House
10 Newington Road
Edinburgh EH9 1QS

9 8 7 6 5 4 3 2 1

www.polygonbooks.co.uk

ISBN 978 1 84697 542 4

British Library Cataloguing-in-Publication Data
A catalogue record for this book is available
from the British Library.

The publisher gratefully acknowledges investment from
Creative Scotland towards the publication of this book.

Typeset in Verdigris MVB by Polygon, Edinburgh
Printed and bound by Gutenberg, Malta

CONTENTS

Introduction   vii

Absence   3
At the Television Set   4
The Beginning   6
By the Fire   7
'Dear man, my love goes
   out in waves'   8
The Divide   10
Floating off to Timor   12
From a City Balcony   15
In Glasgow   17
John 1   19
Love   20
Love and the Worlds   21
One Cigarette   22
The Picnic   23
Smoke   24
Stanzas 6   25
Strawberries   27
The Unspoken   29
A View of Things   32
When You Go   34

INTRODUCTION

Edwin Morgan knew all about love: its mysteries, its silences, its absences, its passion. 'Love is the most mysterious of the winds that blow.'

These poems written over a lifetime, both before and after Morgan came out as gay, seem, above all, necessary. Many of the poems refer to silence – 'they had decided not to talk . . . and then became fearful', giving us a revealing glimpse into Morgan's life and times – and make us realise how much can change during a single lifetime.

There are moments of simple tenderness: the simple act of sharing (perhaps poetry's most famous) strawberries; a lover's cigarette like incense on a balcony; a bus journey home. But, although the lovers come and go, are flighty often, it is the reader who is faithfully present throughout, attendant in this most truthful and universal of poets. Indeed, there is an unsettling feeling we sometimes experience reading a Morgan love poem, that the lover is not giving back in the way that he is being given to – that Morgan needs and wants more, that something is always missing or absent, and that only the reader can fill the gap between. The poems build up an uncommon intimacy on the page, as Morgan credits the reader with understanding more than the lover.

I remember once interviewing Edwin for a radio programme about his love poems. He was talking about Clause 28 and how he felt compelled to come out, but how also being out changed the nature of being in love – that when it was only the two of you who knew, and no one else, there was a power to that. That secrecy, although a negative thing in so many ways, also had its own allure. That conversation struck me with the same force as one that I had years later with Edwin, by then in his old people's home. He was talking about being in love again, and all the feelings being just as fresh as anything. He talked about how liberating it is to have to choose only twelve of your books out of hundreds, and only a few paintings. 'It's good when you have to pare everything down,' he said, 'because when it comes down to it, all that matters is love.' There was something in him that welcomed this simplicity, this return to a certain kind of orderliness, as if his head had more freedom to think interesting thoughts without the clutter.

Morgan's love poems give you a real sense of this shy, passionate, interesting and interested man, a man who is in awe of the elements and of the natural world, as well as the cultural one, a man who appreciates the intensities of absences, and who knows what a power they have on the imagination. The lovers we glimpse from these poems on the whole feel temporary and uncommitted – until we come to the poems about John. It seems then that the poems turn around, it is Morgan who is now apologising for his lateness. It is John who was there all along, unacknowledged and steady, and it is Morgan who feels as if he has appreciated his full worth too late. It is always the way with love – writers through time, from Sappho to Shakespeare to Neruda and beyond, have known the capricious state of love, its temporaneity, its changing face, the way it must be mirrored by the storms, and downpours, the moody skies, the falling leaves, the ways that writers use the marvels of the universe to make sense of love, the constant search to understand it in all its fickleness and fidelities, its faithfulness and deceits. Love unveils the soul. Edwin Morgan felt himself privileged to know this:

> There is so much to say
> And who can delay
> When some are lost and some are seen, our dearest
> heads, and to those and to these we must still
> answer and be true.

It seems apt to end with a quote from 'The Release' – it speaks to us so powerfully: we must still answer and be true.

Jackie Kay

LOVE

ABSENCE

Love is the most mysterious of the winds that blow.
As you lie alone it batters with sleeplessness at the winter
    bedroom window.
The friend is absent, the streetlamp shivers desolately to
    and fro.
Your prostate makes you get up, you look out, police car
    and ambulance howl and flash as they matter-of-factly
    come and go.
There is pain and danger down there, greater than the pain
    you know
        But it is pain all the same
        As you breathe the absent name
Of one who is bonded to you beyond blizzards, time-zones,
    sickness, black stars, snow.

Love and a Life
(Mariscat Press, 2003)

AT THE TELEVISION SET

Take care if you kiss me,
you know it doesn't die.
The lamplight reaches out, draws it
blandly – all of it – into fixity,
troops of blue shadows like the soundless gunfight,
yellow shadows like your cheek by the lamp
where you lie watching, half watching
between the yellow and the blue.
I half see you, half know you.
Take care if you turn now to face me.
For even in this room we are moving out through stars
and forms that never let us back, your hand
lying lightly on my thigh and my hand on your shoulder
are transfixed only there, not here.

What can you bear that would last
like a rock through cancer and white hair?

Yet it is not easy
to take stock of miseries
when the soft light flickers
along our arms in the stillness
where decisions are made.
You have to look at me,
and then it's time that falls
talking slowly to sleep.

From Glasgow to Saturn
(Carcanet Press, 1973)

THE BEGINNING

What potions have I drunk?
Not siren tears, where there was no come-on.
Your presence was enough to make me want
your presence, yet you were the pursuer.
What made you speak to me that night?
It comes in flashes, a hubbub
of Yevtushenko autographs, MacDiarmid
being whisked to his car – Loki in a lounge suit –
the Bute Hall skailing like a swarm of bees,
janitors hovering to shoo us down the stairs
from Babiy Yar and Simbirsk Fair,
and you, a splash of red jeans against the wall
asking me about King Billy till
everything else went out
from my mind and we went out together
into a still cold clear November.
Now nothing is still – I shake.
Nothing is cold – I burn.
Nothing is clear – I toss and turn.
And somehow we've got through December.
Hope brings my fear of the new year.

The New Divan
(Carcanet Press, 1977)

[6]

BY THE FIRE

That night I was your father and mother, I broke
your solitude, I cradled something that you became.
You cried my name.
How wildly we had turned! I smoothed
your brow where we lay in the glow,
kissed you so deep, so long, it was
as if I had moved a key
in the door of desolation,
you were almost weeping
thinking of your dead brother the apple of your eye
crushed in that torn car-metal, your dead sister
grotesque on the black ice, your mother in her grave –
your years of waiting, half life, half death –
your diffidence, your fear –
but I was then your brother and your sister, in
the dance of the fire with your head in my arms.

I will take all the black ice of Lanarkshire
from the heart that only needs love.
What I give you, give me,
and break me free.

Collected Poems
(Carcanet Press, 1990)

[7]

'DEAR MAN, MY LOVE GOES OUT IN WAVES'

Dear man, my love goes out in waves
and breaks. Whatever is, craves.
Terrible the cage
to see all life from, brilliantly about,
crowds, pavements, cars, or hear the common shout
of goals in a near park.
But now the black bars arc
blue in my breath – split – part –
I'm out – it's art,
it's love, it's rage –

Standing in rage in decent air
will never clear the place of care.
Simply to be
should be enough, in the same city, and let
absurd despair tramp and roar off-set.
Be satisfied with it,
the gravel and the grit
the struggling eye can't lift,
the veils that drift,
the weird to dree.

Press close to me at midnight as
you say goodbye; that's what it has
to offer, life
I mean. Into the frost with you; into
the bed with me; and get the light out too.
Better to shake unseen
and let real darkness screen
the shadows of the heart,
the vacant part-
ner, husband, wife.

Themes on a Variation
(Carcanet Press, 1988)

THE DIVIDE

I keep thinking of you – which is ridiculous.
These years between us like a sea.
Any dignity that came with growing older
would stop my pencil on the paper.
The player was open; you asked for the Stones;
got that, got steaming coffee, conversation.
The heavy curtains kept a wild night out.
I keep thinking of your eyes, your hands.
There is no reason for it, none at all.
You would say I can't be what I'm not,
yet I can't not be what I am.
Where does that leave us? What can we do?
The silence after Jagger was like a cloak
I'd have thrown over you – only the wind
was left, and the clocked ticked as you sipped,
clutching the green mug in both hands.
Don't look up suddenly like that!
How hard it is not to watch you.
We had got to the stage of not talking
and not worrying, and that
was almost happy. Then, late,

when you lay on one elbow on the carpet
I could feel nothing but that hot knife
of pain telling me what it was,
and I can't tell you about it, not one word.

The New Divan

(Carcanet Press, 1977)

FLOATING OFF TO TIMOR

If only we'd been strangers
we'd be floating off to Timor,
we'd be shimmering on the Trades
in a blue jersey boat
with shandies, flying fish,
a pace of dolphins
to the copra ports.
And it's no use crying
to me, What dolphins?
I know where they are
and I'd have snapped you up
and carried you away
snapped you up
and carried you away
if we had been strangers.

But here we are care
of the black roofs.
It's not hard to find
with a collar turned up
and a hoot from the Clyde.
The steps come home
whistling too. And a kettle
steams the cranes out slowly.

It's living with ships
makes a rough springtime
and who is safe
when they sing and blow
their music – they seem
to swing at some light rope
like those desires
we keep for strangers.
God, the yellow deck
breathes, it heaves spray
back like a shout.
We're cutting through
some straits of the world
in our old dark room
with salty wings
in the shriek of the dock wind.
But we're caught – meshed
in the fish-scales, ferries,
mudflats, lifebelts
fading into football cries
and the lamps coming on
to bring us in.

We take in
the dream, a cloth from the line
the trains fling sparks on
in our city. We're better awake.
But you know I'd take
you all the same,
if you were my next stranger.

From Glasgow to Saturn
(Carcanet Press, 1973)

FROM A CITY BALCONY

How often when I think of you the day grows bright!
Our silent love
wanders in Glen Fruin with the butterflies and cuckoos –
bring me the drowsy country thing! Let it drift above the traffic
by the open window with a cloud of witnesses –
a sparkling burn, white lambs, the blaze of gorse,
the cuckoos calling madly, the real white clouds over us,
white butterflies about your hand in the short hot grass,
and then the witness was my hand closing on yours,
my mouth brushing your eyelids and your lips
again and again till you sighed and turned for love.
Your breast and thighs were blazing like the gorse.
I covered your great fire in silence there.
We let the day grow old along the grass.
It was in the silence the love was.

Footsteps and witnesses! In this Glasgow balcony who pours
such joy like mountain water? It brims, it spills over and over
down to the parched earth and the relentless wheels.
How often will I think of you, until

our dying steps forget this light, forget
that we ever knew the happy glen,
or that I ever said, We must jump into the sun,
and we jumped into the sun.

The Second Life
(Edinburgh University Press, 1968)

IN GLASGOW

In my smoochy corner
take me on a cloud
I'll wrap you round
and lay you down
in smoky tinfoil
rings and records
sheets of whisky
and the moon all right
old pal all right
the moon all night

Mercy for the rainy
tyres and the violet
thunder that bring you
shambling and shy
from chains of Easterhouse
plains of lights
make your delight
in my nest my spell
my arms and my shell
my barn my bell

I've combed your hair
and washed your feet
and made you turn
like a dark eel
in my white bed
till morning lights
a silent cigarette
throw on your shirt
I lie staring yet
forget forget

From Glasgow to Saturn
(Carcanet Press, 1973)

JOHN I

Nothing will bring him back. I know that, of course I know
  that. The days
When I do not think of him are few, but if I turn my gaze
On a phantom, on a plot of earth, on a faded photograph of
  great times, I raise
Nothing, nearly nothing, no, not nothing, it is the
  something of a pain that stays
Ineradicable and only to be mitigated when I breathe
  the phrase
      I loved you. You must know
      It was truly so, although
As clay in clay you cannot catch my thanks, my steadiness,
  my lateness, my praise.

.

Love and a Life
(Mariscat Press, 2003)

LOVE

Love rules. Love laughs. Love marches. Love is the wolf
 that guards the gate.
Love is the food of music, art, poetry. It fills us and fuels us
 and fires us to create.
Love is terror. Love is sweat. Love is bashed pillow,
 crumpled sheet, unenviable fate.
Love is the honour that kills and saves and nothing will ever
 let that high ambiguity abate.
Love is the crushed ice that tingles and shivers and clinks
 fidgin-fain for the sugar-drenched absinth to fall on it
 and alter its state.
  With love you send a probe
  So far from the globe
No one can name the shoals the voids the belts the zones
 the drags the flares it signals all to leave all and to
 navigate.

Love and a Life
(Mariscat Press, 2003)

LOVE AND THE WORLDS

Scary is this tremulous earth, flaring, shouting, killing and
    being killed.
Is the universe rippling with life? What sign is there that
    space is filled
With anything but gas and dust and fire and rock? Are we
    the tillers to have it tilled?
I think so! And with these red hands, an act of love? Why
    not? We cry but we create, we kill but we build.
Dante was sure the stars were all – even ours – rolled out by
    love. They gild
        A dark that would truly scare
        If there was nothing there
The horror of there not being something, good or bad or
    neither, made or found, willed or self-willed.

Love and a Life
(Mariscat Press, 2003)

[21]

ONE CIGARETTE

No smoke without you, my fire.
After you left,
your cigarette glowed on in my ashtray
and sent up a long thread of such quiet grey
I smiled to wonder who would believe its signal
of so much love. One cigarette
in the non-smoker's tray.
As the last spire
trembles up, a sudden draught
blows it winding into my face.
Is it smell, is it taste?
You are here again, and I am drunk on your tobacco lips.
Out with the light.
Let the smoke lie back in the dark.
Till I hear the very ash
sigh down among the flowers of brass
I'll breathe, and long past midnight, your last kiss.

The Second Life
(Edinburgh University Press, 1968)

THE PICNIC

In a little rainy mist of white and grey
we sat under an old tree,
drank tea toasts to the powdery mountain,
undrunk got merry, played catch
with the empty flask, on the pine needles
came down to where it rolled stealthily away –
you lay
with one arm in the rain, laughing
shaking only your wet hair
loose against the grass, in that enchanted place
of tea, with curtains of a summer rain
dropped round us, for a rainy day.

The Second Life
(Edinburgh University Press, 1968)

SMOKE

I scratch a gap in the curtains:
the darkest morning of the year
goes grey slowly, chains of orange street-lights
lose out east in Glasgow's haze. The smell
of cigarette smoke fills the bedroom. I drown
in it, I gulp you through my lungs again
and hardly find what can be breathed.
Are you destroying me? Or is it a comedy?
To get together naked in a bed, was that all?
To say you had done it? And that we did nothing
was what you had done. Iago and Cassio
had a better night. It must be a laugh
to see us both washed out with lying there.
It doesn't feel like laughing, though,
it feels like gasping, shrieking, tearing, all in silence
as I leave your long curved back
and go through to the kettle and the eggs.

The New Divan
(Carcanet Press, 1977)

The year dissolves in solid days of rain,
runs out, runs off with everything except
you, what you brought me,
gave without having to give, the pain
of the lit fire, the drawn resin that wept.

And I would have nothing other than that.
How the story will end, I cannot see.
You must take stock, take stock!
says the old year. I've scrubbed; shaken the mat;
changed calendars; touch of paint; house, so. But me?

I would have nothing other than what has changed.
You have peeled off some covering, some coat
I thought I needed, when
all I needed was to see it gone, estranged,
not mine, not me. I settled and I wrote

those lines, these lines, only to be true.
Let us be level-headed! With the head?
The head is like a bird,
all quick, hot, hungry, darting through the blue
or two eyes in a rainbush, shivering, unfed –

alive though! We live, we feel, we know
the truth's in feeling, and the openness
feeling must give at last.
Come on then buzz my door and shake the snow
from your padded jacket if January whiteness

drives wetness away; come in; the kettle's on,
the books are out, I die for your look, your talk.
You see how easy I am.
Good God how that Chalk Farm moon knocked and
shone!
Have you not tried my heart? It has no lock.

Themes on a Variation
(Carcanet Press, 1988)

STRAWBERRIES

There were never strawberries
like the ones we had
that sultry afternoon
sitting on the step
of the open french window
facing each other
your knees held in mine
the blue plates in our laps
the strawberries glistening
in the hot sunlight
we dipped them in sugar
looking at each other
not hurrying the feast
for one to come
the empty plates
laid on the stone together
with the two forks crossed
and I bent towards you
sweet in that air
in my arms˙
abandoned like a child
from your eager mouth

the taste of strawberries
in my memory
lean back again
let me love you

let the sun beat
on our forgetfulness
one hour of all
the heat intense
and summer lightning
on the Kilpatrick hills

let the storm wash the plates

The Second Life
(Edinburgh University Press, 1968)

THE UNSPOKEN

When the troopship was pitching round the Cape
in '41, and there was a lull in the night uproar of seas and
    winds, and a sudden full moon
swung huge out of the darkness like the world it is,
and we all crowded onto the wet deck, leaning on the rail,
    our arms on each other's shoulders, gazing at the savage
    outcrop of great Africa,
and Tommy Cosh started singing 'Mandalay' and we joined in
    with our raucous chorus of the unforgettable song,
and the dawn came up like thunder like that moon drawing
    the water of our yearning
though we were going to war, and left us exalted,
that was happiness,
but it is not like that.

When the television newscaster said
the second sputnik was up, not empty
but with a small dog on board,
a half-ton treasury of life orbiting a thousand miles above
    the thin television masts and mists of November,
in clear space, heard, observed,
the faint far heartbeat sending back its message

steady and delicate,
and I was stirred by a deep confusion of feelings,
got up, stood with my back to the wall and my palms
    pressed hard against it, my arms held wide
as if I could spring from this earth –
not loath myself to go out that very day where Laika had
    shown man,
felt my cheeks burning with old Promethean warmth
rekindled – ready –
covered my face with my hands, seeing only an animal
strapped in a doomed capsule, but the future
was still there, cool and whole like the moon,
waiting to be taken, smiling even
as the dog's bones and the elaborate casket of aluminium
glow white and fuse in the arc of re-entry,
and I knew what I felt was history,
its thrilling brilliance came down,
came down,
comes down on us all, bringing pride and pity,
but it is not like that.

But Glasgow days and grey weather, when the rain
beat on the bus shelter and you leaned slightly against me,
    and the back of your hand touched my hand in the
    shadows, and nothing was said,

when your hair grazed mine accidentally as we talked in
    a café, yet not quite accidentally,
when I stole a glance at your face as we stood in a doorway
    and found I was afraid
of what might happen if I should never see it again,
when we met, and met, in spite of such differences in our
    lives,
and did the common things that in our feeling
became extraordinary, so that our first kiss
was like the winter morning moon, and as you shifted in
    my arms
it was the sea changing the shingle that changes it
as if for ever (but we are bound by nothing, but like smoke
to mist or light in water we move, and mix) –
O then it was a story as old as war or man,
and although we have not said it we know it,
and although we have not claimed it we do it,
and although we have not vowed it we keep it,
without a name to the end.

The Second Life

(Edinburgh University Press, 1968)

A VIEW OF THINGS

what I love about dormice is their size
what I hate about rain is its sneer
what I love about the Bratach Gorm is its unflappability
what I hate about scent is its smell
what I love about newspapers is their etaoin shrdl
what I hate about philosophy is its pursed lip
what I love about Rory is his old grouse
what I hate about Pam is her pinkie
what I love about semi-precious stones is their preciousness
what I hate about diamonds is their mink
what I love about poetry is its ion engine
what I hate about hogs is their setae
what I love about love is its porridge-spoon
what I hate about hate is its eyes
what I love about hate is its salts
what I hate about love is its dog
what I love about Hank is his string vest
what I hate about the twins is their three gloves
what I love about Mabel is her teeter
what I hate about gooseberries is their look, feel, smell,
    and taste

what I love about the world is its shape
what I hate about a gun is its lock, stock, and barrel
what I love about bacon-and-eggs is its predictability
what I hate about derelict buildings is their reluctance to
    disintegrate
what I love about a cloud is its unpredictability
what I hate about you, chum, is your china
what I love about many waters is their inability to quench
    love

The Second Life
(Edinburgh University Press, 1968)

WHEN YOU GO

When you go,
if you go,
and I should want to die,
there's nothing I'd be saved by
more than the time
you fell asleep in my arms
in a trust so gentle
I let the darkening room
drink up the evening, till
rest, or the new rain
lightly roused you awake.
I asked if you heard the rain in your dream
and half dreaming still you only said, I love you.

The Second Life
(Edinburgh University Press, 1968)

ABOUT THE AUTHOR

EDWIN MORGAN (1920–2010) was born in Glasgow, and spent his life there except for his six years with the Royal Army Medical Corps in the Middle East. He studied English Literature at the University of Glasgow, where he went on to teach, retiring as Professor Emeritus in 1980. He was appointed Glasgow's Poet Laureate in 1999, and awarded the Queen's Gold Medal for Poetry in 2000. In 2004 he was appointed the first Scots Makar of modern times, and wrote the poem 'For the Opening of the Scottish Parliament' in the same year. His poetry is praised for its linguistic inventiveness, social realism and humane curiosity. He wrote concrete and visual poetry, opera libretti and collaborated with jazz saxophonist Tommy Smith to set his work to music; he was also a translator, playwright and critic. Morgan's work is renowned for its outward-looking internationalism, his poetic gaze moving from Europe to the wider world and into space, yet always returning to Glasgow, whose people and landscape he so memorably evoked and imagined.